Find Magic & Find Joy
The Original Mommy-and-Me
Coloring and Seek-and-Find Journal!

To Brian
and our
five pairs of chickens
four sons
three cats
two dogs
one amazing life!

©2021 by Bright Communications LLC
All rights reserved. No part of this publication may be reproduced or transmitted in any form or by any means, electronic or mechanical, including photocopying, recording, or any other information storage and retrieval system, without the written permission of the publisher.
Printed in the United States of America
Published in Hellertown, PA
Cover and illustrations by Anna Magruder
ISBN 978-1-952481-78-9
2 4 6 8 10 9 7 5 3 1 paperback

For more information or to place bulk orders, contact the publisher at Jennifer@BrightCommunications.net.

BrightCommunications.net

Mom coloring pages are on the left!

What's your favorite way to spend time with your flock?

_____
_____
_____
_____

Kid coloring pages are on the right!

What's your favorite way to spend time with your flock?

_____
_____
_____
_____

Where do you go to get some space?

_____
_____
_____
_____

Where do you go to get some space?

_____
_____
_____
_____

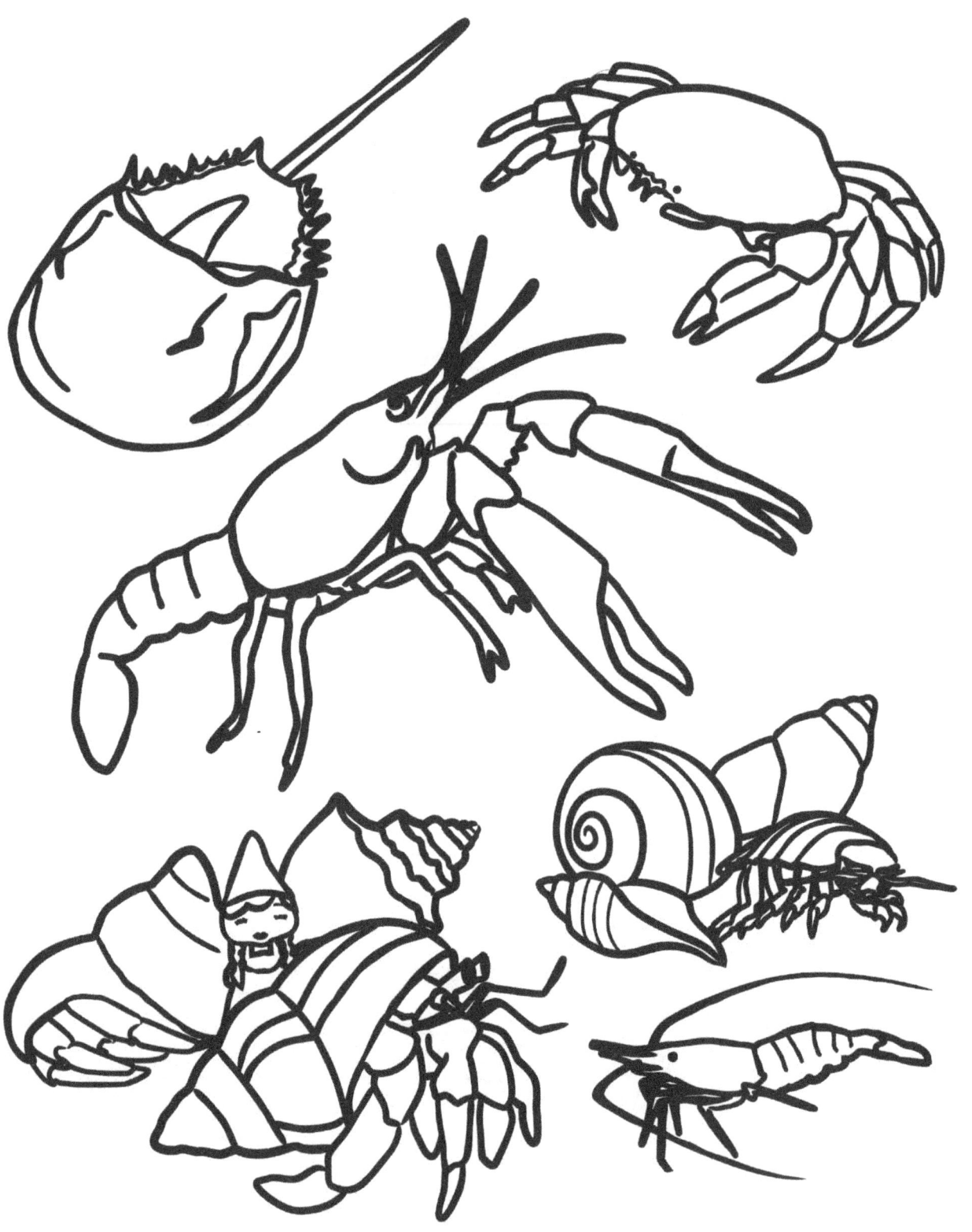

What do you do when you feel a little crabby?

_____
_____
_____
_____

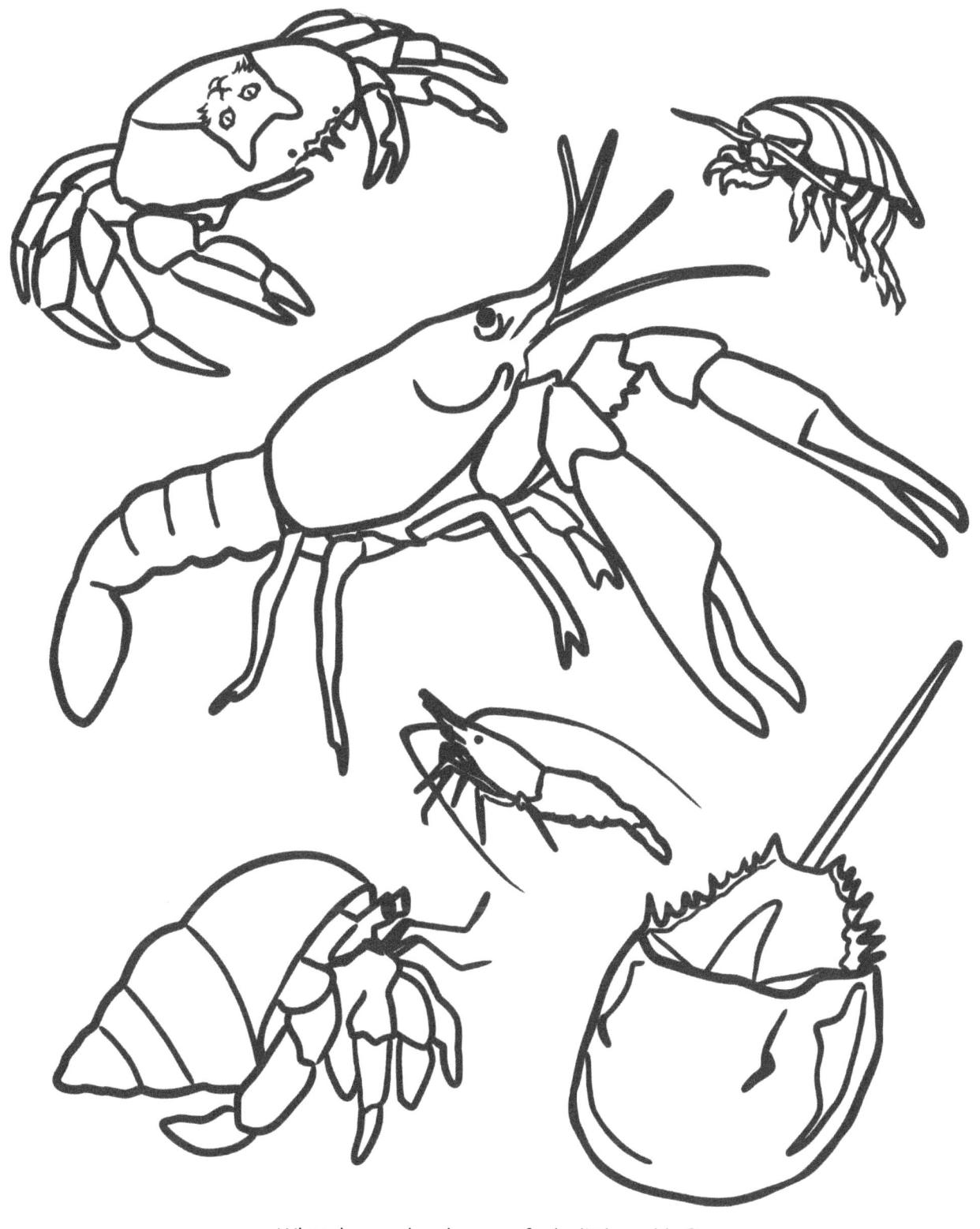

What do you do when you feel a little crabby?

_____
_____
_____
_____

What makes you feel most free?

_____
_____
_____
_____

What makes you feel most free?

_____
_____
_____
_____

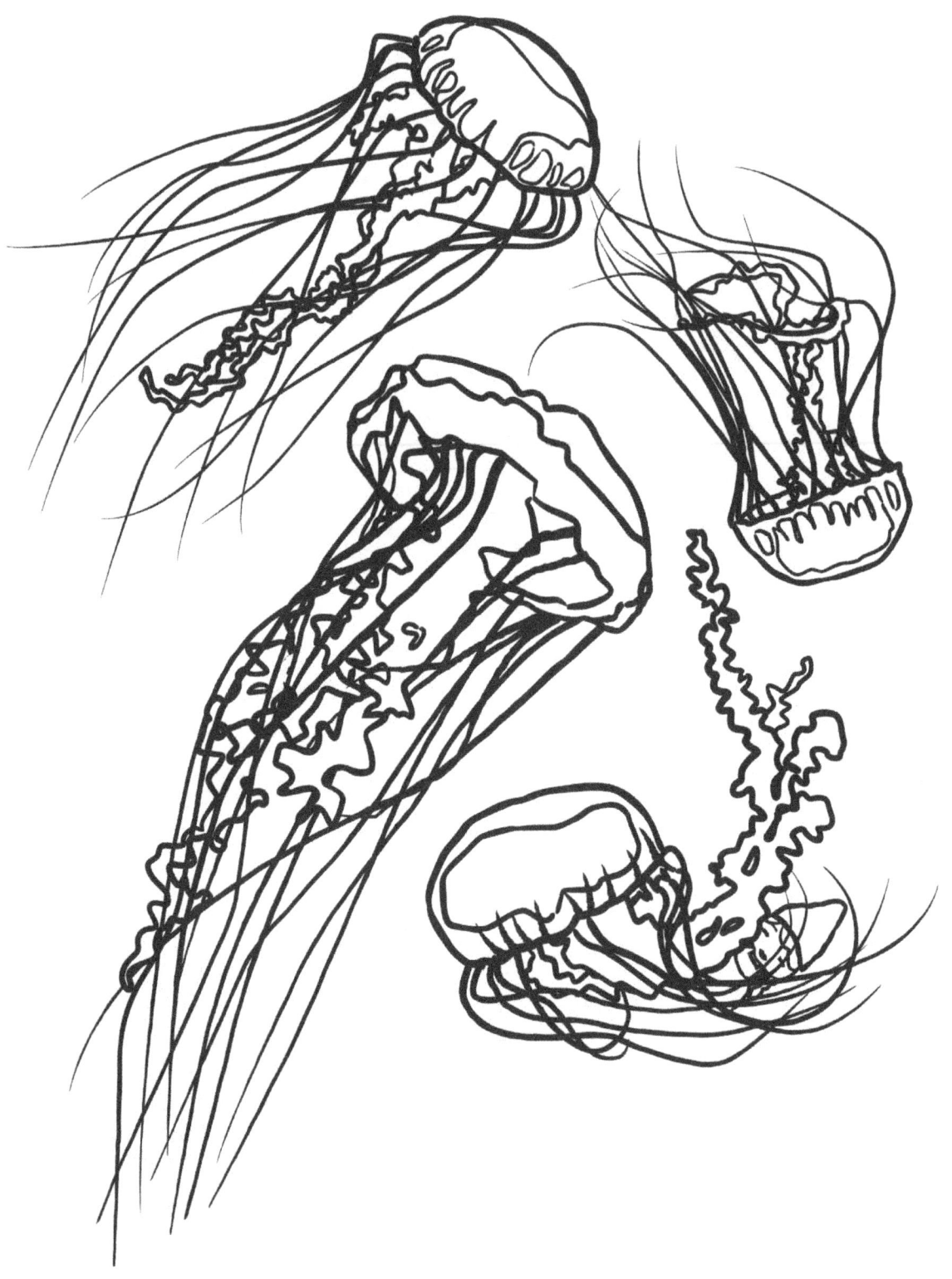

What is your favorite way to play?

_____
_____
_____
_____

What is your favorite way to play?

_____
_____
_____
_____

When do you soar?

When do you soar?

_____
_____
_____
_____

How does your light shine?

_____
_____
_____
_____

How does your light shine?
___
___
___
___

When do you wish you had eight hands to get more done?

_____
_____
_____
_____

When do you wish you had eight hands to get more done?

_____
_____
_____
_____

What lights your inner fire?

_____
_____
_____
_____

What lights your inner fire?
_____
_____
_____
_____

Do you swim with the crowd or do your own thing?

_____
_____
_____
_____

Do you swim with the crowd or do your own thing?

_____
_____
_____
_____

How do you relax and recharge?

_____
_____
_____
_____

How do you relax and recharge?

_____
_____
_____
_____

What makes you flip?

_____
_____
_____
_____

What makes you flip?

_____
_____
_____
_____

How do you horse around?

_____
_____
_____
_____

How do you horse around?

_____
_____
_____
_____

What makes you feel cozy and safe?

_____
_____
_____
_____

What makes you feel cozy and safe?
_____
_____
_____
_____

How do you avoid life's sharks?

_____
_____
_____
_____

How do you avoid life's sharks?

_____
_____
_____
_____

When do you spend time surrounded by nature?

_____
_____
_____
_____

When do you spend time surrounded by nature?

_____
_____
_____
_____

How do you keep all life's balls in the air?

_____
_____
_____
_____

How do you keep all life's balls in the air?

_____
_____
_____
_____

What exciting places do you want to visit?
_____
_____
_____
_____

What exciting places do you want to visit?

_____
_____
_____
_____

What makes you feel in the flow?

_____
_____
_____
_____

What makes you feel in the flow?

_____
_____
_____
_____

What are your biggest dreams?

_____
_____
_____
_____

What are your biggest dreams?

_____
_____
_____
_____

About Bright Communications

Bright Communications LLC is a woman- and veteran-owned custom publisher in the Lehigh Valley, Pennsylvania. Jennifer Bright founded Bright Communications LLC in 2004, fueled by her love of books and helping people.

Over the years, the company has grown from a one-woman business providing editorial services to other publishing companies to a robust organization employing more than 25 independent professionals and publishing more than 35 books a year in most book categories, including fiction, health, inspiration, parenting, memoir, and children's books.

Our efficient, effective process takes authors from ideas all the way through to finished books. We create print, eBook, and audiobook editions, and our books are available everywhere books are sold.

Our passion is helping authors and brands bring their books to life.

We make publishing easy—and fun!

Eighty-five percent of people say they have a book in them!
Do you?
Let us help you bring your book to life!

Contact: Jennifer Bright
jennifer@brightcommunications.net
610-216-0913
Mention this ad for 10% off our publishing packages!

CPSIA information can be obtained
at www.ICGtesting.com
Printed in the USA
BVHW052003040122
625366BV00015B/705